Rookie Read-About Geography

WITHDRAWN

Europe

by Rebecca Hirsch

Content Consultant
Judith Otto
Assistant Professor of Geography
Framingham State University

Reading Consultant
Jeanne Clidas
Reading Specialist

Children's Press®
An Imprint of Scholastic Inc.
New York • Toronto • London • Auckland • Sydney • Mexico City
New Delhi • Hong Kong • Danbury, Connecticut

Library of Congress Cataloging-in-Publication Data
Hirsch, Rebecca E.
  Europe / by Rebecca Hirsch.
     p. cm. – (Rookie read-about geography)
  Includes index.
  ISBN 978-0-531-28979-2 (lib.bdg.) – ISBN 978-0-531-29279-2
(pbk.)
  1. Europe–Juvenile literature. 2. Europe–Geography–Juvenile
literature. I. Title.

  D1051.H57 2012
  940–dc23

                          2012013404

SCHOLASTIC, CHILDREN'S PRESS, ROOKIE READ-ABOUT®,
and associated logos are trademarks and/or registered trademarks of
Scholastic Inc.

1 2 3 4 5 6 7 8 9 10 R 22 21 20 19 18 17 16 15 14 13

Photographs © 2013: Alamy Images: 26 (Hemis), cover background (Igor
Kisselev), 12 (Peter Phipp/Travelshots.com), 14 (Stefano Politi Markovina),
16, 31 bottom right (Terry Smith Images); Corbis Images/Ian Langsdon/
epa: 10; Getty Images: 18, 31 top right (Marco Brivio), 29 (Sami Sarkis);
Photo Researchers/Pierre Vernay: 20, 31 top left; Shutterstock, Inc.: cover
left inset (Daniel Gale), cover right inset (Iakov Kalinin), 30 (raphme);
Superstock, Inc.: 24, 31 bottom left (age fotostock), 8 (imagebroker.net),
22 (Nordic Photos).

Maps by Matt Kania/www.maphero.com

Table of Contents

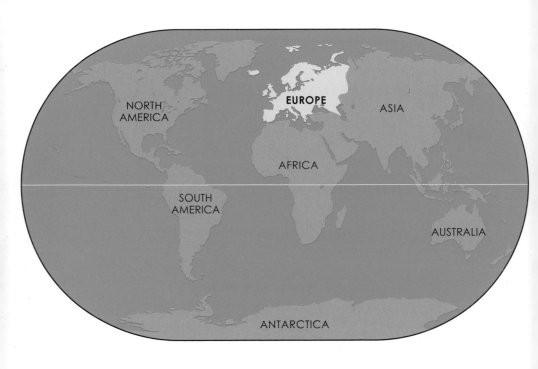

NORTH
AMERICA

EUROPE

ASIA

AFRICA

SOUTH
AMERICA

AUSTRALIA

ANTARCTICA

The seven continents map

4

Welcome to Europe!

Europe is a continent. The largest pieces of land on Earth are continents. There are seven. Europe is the yellow continent on this map.

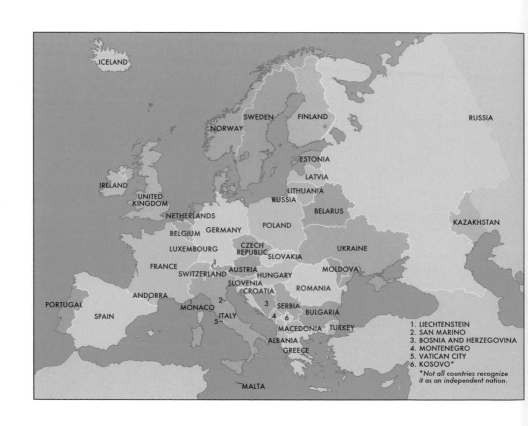

ICELAND

NORWAY SWEDEN FINLAND RUSSIA

ESTONIA
LATVIA
IRELAND LITHUANIA
UNITED RUSSIA
KINGDOM BELARUS KAZAKHSTAN
NETHERLANDS POLAND
BELGIUM GERMANY
LUXEMBOURG CZECH
REPUBLIC UKRAINE
SLOVAKIA
FRANCE 1 AUSTRIA MOLDOVA
SWITZERLAND HUNGARY
SLOVENIA
ANDORRA CROATIA ROMANIA
PORTUGAL 2
MONACO 3 SERBIA
ITALY 4 6 BULGARIA
SPAIN 5 MACEDONIA TURKEY
ALBANIA
GREECE

MALTA

1. LIECHTENSTEIN
2. SAN MARINO
3. BOSNIA AND HERZEGOVINA
4. MONTENEGRO
5. VATICAN CITY
6. KOSOVO*
*Not all countries recognize
it as an independent nation.

Map of Europe

6

Europe is a small continent, but it has many countries. Germany, Spain, and Italy are three countries in Europe. Can you find them on this map?

Children dance at Oktoberfest in Bavaria, Germany.

People of Europe

Each country has its own language, foods, and customs. In Germany, people speak German. They celebrate a festival called Oktoberfest.

10   Prince William and the Duchess of Cambridge
on their wedding day in the United Kingdom

In the United Kingdom, people speak English. The United Kingdom has a royal family.

People riding boats in Venice, Italy

In Italy, people speak Italian. There is a city in Italy where the streets are waterways. There are no cars. People walk on sidewalks or ride boats to go from place to place.

A colorful dragon fountain in Barcelona, Spain

14

Places to See

There are many things to see in Europe. People visit the beautiful parks and buildings in the cities.

Schoolchildren at a museum in France

They visit Europe's museums to see art. There are famous paintings in the museums.

18 The Egeskov castle in Denmark has water all around it.

They come to see castles that were built long ago.

A brown bear looks for food in a forest in Finland.

Land and Water

Europe has forests. Trees grow in the forests and many animals live there.

People picking grapes off the vines in France

Europe has places that are hot and dry. The weather is good for growing olives and grapes.

Children ski in the Alps in Italy.

Europe has mountains. It has groups of mountains called ranges. The tallest mountain range in Europe is the Alps.

A boat on the Danube River in Budapest, Hungary

Europe has many rivers. The rivers connect cities to the sea. Visitors travel on the rivers to see Europe's interesting places.

Modern Marvels

- The Millau Viaduct stretches across a deep valley in France.

- It is the world's tallest bridge!

- The bridge has tall columns and cables. The columns and cables work together to hold up the bridge.

Try It!

Can you find the triangle shapes in this bridge? What parts help the bridge stand up? If you built a bridge, what would it look like?

Meet an Alpine Ibex

- Alpine ibexes are wild goats.

- They live high in the mountains in Europe.

- These goats are excellent climbers.

Words You Know

bear

castle

mountain

museum

Index

Facts for Now

Visit this Scholastic Web site for more information on Europe:
www.factsfornow.scholastic.com
Enter the keyword **Europe**

About the Author

Rebecca Hirsch is a scientist-turned-writer and the author of many books for young readers.

[5]